SHERWIN WASHINGTON

STATIC

HOW TO HEAR YOUR SECRET CALL FROM GOD

© Copyright 2022 - All Rights Reserved.
ISBN - 9798423259518
Written by **Sherwin Washington**

The contents of this book may not be reproduced, duplicated or transmitted without direct written permission from the author.

Under no circumstances will any legal responsibility or blame be held against the publisher for any reparation, damages, or monetary loss due to the information herein, either directly or indirectly.

<u>Legal Notice:</u>

This book is copyright protected. This is only for personal use. You cannot amend, distribute, sell, use, quote or paraphrase any part or the content within this book without the consent of the author.

Acknowledgement

The steps of a good man are ordered, and I want to first acknowledge God who knew me before I was formed in my mother's womb. When I stepped into this world, my path was already blessed and highly favored by him. Secondly, I want to acknowledge my mother, Annette Washington. You were the first step God ordered to introduce me to love and the Bible. Because of you, I learned that there is a difference between red and black writings as a child. I asked you why it is so much red in the middle of the Bible, and you responded, "because Jesus is talking". With no real understanding, God used you back then to help me recognize him differently. Even if it was just the colors in words. Thirdly, I want to acknowledge my bride, Quineshia Washington. God gave me a glimpse of my future wife back in our puppy love days of Jr High. God always kept a place in my heart just for you, and your love pulled me out of the world I strayed away in. You were the one he used to clear up the confusion of what I thought love was. You were the bridge God used to connect me back from darkness to light. You were concerned about why I stopped attending a church, and I told you I didn't know what to believe.

You helped my faith by watching yours, and I always felt I was lucky to catch a woman like you but realized God used you to catch a man like me. You were the step I needed to walk me right into my fourth acknowledgement: my home church, Wilmington Missionary Baptist Church. To the leader of the house, Reverend Joey Horton Sr., God used you to be a perfect example of what a leader looks like. A man after Gods own heart is who you are. Wilmington family, you accepted my family and me with much love and watched me grow. Every one of you made an impact on my life. I want to thank you for keeping me grounded in the word and teaching me the truth about God. Because of you, I grew from that shy boy in the back of the church, to speaking publicly in front of the church. I no longer see myself the same. Even though it was hard to see me go, look at me as your child leaving the nest. I was spiritually raised well because of you, and I'm finding my own way.

May God continue to bless every one of you, and remember I love you, and there's nothing you can do about it.

CONTENTS

Introduction 1

Chapter One 7
    The Call

Chapter Two 17
    What It Sounds Like

Chapter Three 25
    A Familiar Voice

Chapter Four 35
    Visitations Are Closed

Chapter Five 45
    What's In Your Hands

Chapter Six 55
    Call It In The Air

Chapter Seven 67
    Cut It Out

Chapter Eight 77
    I Want Out

INTRODUCTION

It's 3:45 in the morning; my picture is being taken. My finger and hands are being scanned. I take a shower and get dressed in a jumpsuit and head out the door. I scanned the room and watched the entrance where different people came into the building and went through the same check-in process. It's a lot of people in here, but I feel alone. Some people are coming in angry and cursing, some sweaty, and shirts are ripped up. A few people are banging on the doors screaming at the top of their lungs. A thought surfaced in my mind, saying, "how did I get here"? The lonely feeling crept in because nobody even knew where I was right now. I am about 250 miles away from my home, and I can't believe I ended up here. But I knew exactly how I ended up here; I had some fake friends tagging along with me for a while that got me caught up in this mess. But I know I have some hope left; I have my one phone call.

After being processed, I asked a guard, "can I have my phone call now?" Rudely responding, he said, "you have 5 minutes, and you're headed to the back". The first person I thought of dialling was mama—the phone rang and rang and rang. No answer. I dialled again and again, still no response. "Why isn't she picking up?" my thought. "She can't be sleeping that hard". Have you ever tried to get in touch with somebody and can't seem to reach them? Especially in an emergency? How did you feel about it? How do you reach someone who doesn't even know where you are? You've taken the wrong road and ended up in a dead-end situation.

The only hope I have now is to pray; maybe God will hear me and help somehow. It's funny when we're out in the world doing our things; we tend to forget about God until something happens. Or until we get some bad news and then we remember to pray or ask him for help. When sickness drops or the grim reaper threatens us, we quickly run to the church and pray on alters. Instead of talking and then walking away from your prayers, have you ever thought about listening? Hearing and listening are two different things. You hear with your ear, but you listen with your heart. "Wisdom takes stands in the top of highest places, by the way in the places of paths, wisdom speaks at the gates of the city entrance", according to Proverbs 8:2-3. However, we tend to have a hard time listening to it. Static is a book that weighed on my heart to write based on the story of Job in the Bible and my own experiences.

Bible scholars say it's one of the oldest books written in the Bible. It's one of the wisdom-based books and tells a story of a righteous man who lost everything life could offer. To me, the book is depressing. I hated to hear a sermon about Job because I always felt so negative about him losing everything he had. My mindset was trying to gain everything he had, like most people in life. Most people want to model Mr. and Mrs. Jones in life, and Job's story shows how it was all taken away. I didn't want to hear anything about the book of Job. But little did I know the very thing I ran from was what I was going to need. Like Job's story, I had to learn to pass the first few pages and read the rest.

The introduction was based on my true-life story that I'm not proud of, but I've gained wisdom from it. I also need to get over my past by sharing some light with you and continuing my story. I indeed had some fake friends hanging around me at the time that landed me in jail, but they couldn't get me out. I'm not ashamed to reveal their names in this book: George, Abraham, Alexander, Andrew, Ulysses, and Benjamin. Yeah, all of them were fake because I had counterfeit money in my possession. We all have real friends and fake friends in life. But in this situation, I loved my fake friends and their company in my presence. What I had to learn about them was that getting caught with counterfeit money is a serious federal crime, and I was facing that reality. The first lesson I learned is: money talks and walks. Sometimes it walks right out of your pockets, and other times, it walks you right in the doors of the prison. Hard lesson to learn.

I'm telling this story to guide you in a direction. In the book of Job, he also had friends who came around while he was going through his issues. Job 33:14 reads, "God speaks once, yea twice, yet man perceives it not". If God speaks, then how does he sound? When does he speak and am I able to hear him? Can you hear the voice of God, and do you know when he speaks? Do you know the sound of Gods voice? When you pray, do you do all the talking only? Why does it seem so hard to reach God?

The good thing about my life story is I do have good friends I can talk with, and some are believers in Christ. I can remember a conversation I was having about the same problem of not hearing God. I was going through some things and was praying a lot but felt frustrated because I wasn't getting a response. In the middle of the conversation, my friend interrupted me and said God just spoke to him, saying, "I hear you; I've heard you, but do you hear me?" From that point on, my journey began with listening and following the voice of God. When he speaks, it's for a reason, but you must learn to listen to him. The hard part is the statics of life usually distract us from hearing what he's trying to say or even recognizing if he's speaking at all.

One of the main Statics I see is the love of money. Or, in my case, "friends" that were around me. Maybe God is calling you, but you don't understand his voice or recognize what he's saying because of the statics in your life. He may be calling to stop you in your tracks or maybe trying to get you out of a situation. Whatever it is, let me be a friend to you and share my experience to help you tune in on how he speaks and what he may be saying to you.

CHAPTER ONE

The Call

Living in-between times of communication is a little different from how I grew up and how it is now. Technology has advanced phones to do more than just talk in today's times. We have the luxury of accessing the internet, text communication, live video chats, and even shooting films with phones now. But I still remember growing up in the time of landline phones in houses. The younger generations probably don't understand what I'm referring to. These types of phones were connected to outlets on the walls. Yes, the old-school phones with cords could trip you off if you don't watch your step across the floors. The same phones you couldn't sneak in a room without anybody noticing the white cord trailing under the doors. When the phone rings, you don't know who's calling until you pick it up. Imagine living in those times again. Think of the inconvenience of you sitting comfortably on the couch, watching television, and dozing off to sleep. Suddenly, the phone rings and wakes you up from your sleep - we all know the best sleep is the one you dozed off. But this annoying phone is now ringing in another room. If you care to answer, you will be forced to get up from your chair, run to the phone and answer it before it stops ringing.

Looking back at those times, I've noticed that answering a call is a process. Let me explain some key principles of a call. First, you're in one comfortable place, and you recognize a sound in another place. Next, you must get out of your comfortable place and follow the location's sound. Once you've found the location of the call, you must answer the call before the ring stops. So, there is a time limit involved. Although it may be easier to catch the call in the familiarity of your own home, however, let's say you're in an unfamiliar house. If I invite you to stay at my house for a night and permit you to answer any calls that come through, how fast can you get to the call before it stops? The same situation applies; you dozed off to sleep, awakening by a call, and have a limited time to answer the call before it stops. Do you see the principles?

From what I experienced with God and callings, I also looked back in my time and in times of the Bible when he called man. To better understand how to answer a calling, you must know the language of what's trying to be communicated. For example, when the phone is ringing, the phone itself is speaking loudly, saying, "Get up out your sleep, come here to where I am, and listen to who it is". We know what to do when the phone rings because we've grown to learn the language of a phone. But some of us are still asleep and don't recognize the language of God's calling. Think of a baby sleeping peacefully in a room, and suddenly, the phone rings. Initially, the ringing will wake the baby out of sleep, and he/she begins to cry. To hear the calling, recognize what's ringing the loudest in your life? In other words, what seems to be the most disturbance in your spirit/soul? What's trying to get your attention and you're procrastinating on? That's usually a sign because you've gotten comfortable in a situation or a place in life, and now it seems to be a force or a push to get up and do something.

So, now we see that the first step is to wake up from our sleep. Let me address this, sleep in the Bible sometimes means dead. Being spiritually dead requires rising and accepting and being saved by Christ. Acknowledge that you are a sinner by confessing with your mouth and asking for forgiveness. Believe with your heart that Jesus Christ died for you. Now, just like a newborn baby, it's alive but often sleeps a lot. So, you may have accepted Christ before, but nothing much has changed. Maybe you don't recognize any difference in your life. You've become a born-again believer, but what does that mean now? A baby cries because its sleep was disturbed, and he doesn't know what to do about the noise he's hearing. You may be hearing something in the spirit, but you don't know how to respond. Have you ever noticed anything unusual around you lately? Any disturbance going on inside of you? Before I came to Christ, my wife recognized the call and the ringing around me to which I was dead. She was already a believer, but I was sleeping in my own ways of life. I didn't care about going to a church, reading the Bible, or even praying to bless my food. But because she already had a relationship with God, not being in a church bothered her soul. She already recognized some minor signs around me the whole time. For instance, my car had a cross on the front tag that I never paid attention to. My calendar had a cross at the top of it in my Big Rig that I never paid attention to. I had a brand-new Bible around me, but I only liked it because my name was written on the front cover in gold italic letters. It was a gift to me from a church I attended at a young age, but I never bothered to read it. I never understood why I even kept that Bible around. I can laugh now, but I took care of that Bible, and I still have it today.

My wife's awareness of it seemed like I couldn't escape these signs from God everywhere I went. She recognized it, but I didn't. I didn't even care because it could've been all a coincidence to me. As time went on, I didn't mind going to church, but that every Sunday thing was starting to get on my nerves. My wife was starting to bother my sleep, in other words. She became the disturbance and the most ringing phone in my ears. Sweetheart, I know you may be reading this, but I must inform the people that you were the loudest ringing in my ears. I was comfortable hanging out late Saturday nights and sleeping on Sunday mornings. I was comfortable sipping my special beverages with my friends. I was comfortable with the foul language and places of interest I had in my spirit. She was starting to be sickening with this whole idea about the church and God thing. In my own words, "will somebody else please get the phone"!

Your loudest ring may be the closest person to you or maybe the closest thing to you—the closest thing meaning what's calling for your attention. Let's say the phone rings, and you don't bother to answer it. I can guarantee you that it will ring again and again, and again until it annoys you so much that you will start to get frustrated with it. Anger will build up inside your because you know you must answer it. If you haven't noticed yet, start to pay attention to life problems that aggravate you the most. Problems in the world you have the passion for fixing. A passion is anything in your heart that you have strong emotions for. Anything that gets you fired up, and you say somebody needs to do something about this! That somebody may be you. If a problem seems to bring awareness to your soul constantly, then that's an important call. Start to be aware of the noise in your life. As I explained, ringing is another language meaning, come here. The ringing is noise to the ear, and you must get to the location to stop it. It may be time for you to get up out of your comfortable sleep and figure out where is "here". To understand this principle, follow the noise. Whatever is causing pressure to you is the noise in your ear. Pressure forces you to move and do something you don't feel like doing. If you naturally feel pressure in the ear, you go somewhere to see a doctor and stop it.

I felt a little pressure to start going to church consistently, which finally led me to open and read the Bible I always had. The first book of Genesis explains what God did at the beginning of creation and how he created man. The first man created was Adam.

God created Adam with abilities. Adam, to me, is the blueprint on what our original state of being was supposed to be. Adam probably had the perfect body. Every muscle showing and six-pack abs that everyman works to have now. Adam ate the best foods for the health of the body. Adam had no blood pressure issues, no high cholesterol, no diabetes, no sickness, or diseases. There was no such thing as death or fear. Adam was in a perfect relationship with God, with no static to hear him when he speaks. Adam was built as a Man with no childhood issues. Adam had it made in the shade. God gave Adam business principles to flourish the earth. Genesis 1:28 says, "He blessed them, and to be fruitful, multiply, replenish, subdue, and have dominion over the earth". God designed the workplace environment for Adam before he was even brought to it. It reads in Genesis 2:8, "And the Lord God planted a garden eastward in Eden; and there he put the man whom he had formed". Eastward is the important clue. It represents the exact location for the garden to flourish. When planting a garden, it must be in the right location for the sun, it must be near some water, and have enough space to grow.

The sun rises in the east, so the garden must be in a position where nothing is blocking the light source for at least six hours a day. God had a mainstream river flowing through Eden, which means a water source must be close by for dry times. And the ground must be rich with fertile soil for the seeds to take root. The garden requires a special person who has knowledge and abilities to manage the ground, and Adam was that person. Adam was a professional farmer and a gardener and was able to take care of the garden with his natural abilities. No tools were given to him to help him get the job done. God created him as the tool for the garden. He did not have to take farming classes. He did not have to learn how to be a gardener. CEO was built inside of him from the beginning. That's why the Word said he blessed them first before he said, "Be fruitful and multiply". This was all in the designed plans of God in the beginning. But as we know, plans change depending on situations. Adam was married in the right location, but the drama in the garden made him sin and caused him to cover himself up, run, and hide from God. God called for him, and Adam began to hear the ringing. Genesis 3:9, "And the Lord God called to Adam, and said unto him, where are you?"

Adam was in the right location and had a job to do, but the drama and the guilt of sin made him cover up who he was really created to be. Adam was living with a false identity of himself, and God was saying come "here". To hear the calling of God, you first must come "here". Here is where God is. Here is his Word in the Bible. Here is inside the local church to hear his Word being taught.

Here is first presenting yourself to him as you are. You see, ever since the curse of sin came into humanity, we must reverse the process of knowing who God is and knowing who we are before we could ever know where our own location in life could be. We've lost our identity, and answering the ringing is the only way to hear our true identity. I never would've seen any of this had I not been in the right location.

To sum all these up, the call of God is recognizing a ring in our lives, coming to him, and then becoming who we were really created to be. It's a journey, but you must take the first step. The pressure to answer my own call led me to come into the church, open the Bible, and see what all these mean. I was in the right location to answer the phone call, but I had to study my sources before I was sent out to grow in my own garden. My ground was rich in the spirit of love from other believers who helped me grow in the space I needed. I had enough sunlight from the knowledge and teachings I received from coming to the Word consistently. And because I was sowing my time, the water blessings of income sustained me in my life. God provides all the sources needed, and I want you to see these and understand these principles so you can recognize a call and direction in your life. You were created to do something and become someone totally different from what you're accustomed to. That's the real journey and real location God wants you to reach in your life, but it all starts with recognizing and answering the call. Remember there's a time limit to answer a phone call before it stops ringing, and that time limit is your life.

CHAPTER TWO
What It Sounds Like

The definitions of sound from the Oxford Dictionary are:
1. *"Vibrations that travel through the air or another medium and can be heard when they reach a person's or animal's ear;"*
2. *"Sound produced by continuous and regular vibrations, as opposed to noise".*

A sound originates from a source and travels to the ear to be heard. For example, during a thunderstorm, the loud rumbles and the booms originate from the activity that's going on in the atmosphere. We can feel the effects of how loud it is by the vibrations of windows in the house or the hallow echoes from the wooden floors. Most of our children fear the noise of thunderstorms, but they don't understand what's going on. Static electricity flashes followed by a loud sonic boom seconds later would startle anyone when it's not expected. From my own experience as a child, Grandma would take a thunderstorm seriously but not in a way that we usually think in terms of safety. No, her seriousness was based on letting God speak. I can remember her yelling at us now because we would laugh, run, and hide every time we saw flashes and heard the rumbles. In her words, "hush your mouth and sit down while the lord is speaking!"

As a child, it's all just fun and games to us. However, I did notice how everything was turned off and how I was forced to be still until the storm blew over. My thoughts were, "I guess God has finished talking now, huh, Grandma?" I never bothered to ask her what he said. Or better still, what kind of language is he even speaking because I don't understand a thing. If you have only learned one language your whole life, try and converse with someone else who speaks another language. I guarantee you won't get along with each other. But what I realized now; is it was not different when I've gotten older. Most people still don't understand what God sounds like and what he may be saying. I've grown to hear people say all the time God told them this or God said that, or some don't even believe he speaks at all. Some people in the church itself can't grasp the idea of God speaking audibly again or what he even sounds like.

Bible scholars and commentaries say we have the finished books of the Bible, and God doesn't speak that way anymore. Well, I am here to inform you that the problem is not God; he's still the same yesterday, today and forever. The problem is people and their opinions of what other people say and think. I'll prove what I'm saying in the Gospel Book of John 12:29 reads, "The crowd of people who were standing there heard the sound of this voice, they said that it was like the noise of thunder in a storm. But other people said an angel spoke to him!" I believe there are levels of hearing. Being seasoned in age, my grandma had a closer relationship with God than I had. She must've learned how to discern His sound, different from the noise I was receiving in my ears. I represented the crowd of people that only heard the rumble. My grandma represented the people that heard the voice of an Angel. The problem is that people are standing in the same location on earth but have different opinions on what's being communicated in the air. We hear natural things with our natural ears, like thunderstorms. In contrast, we hear spiritual things with our spiritual's ears, like the voice of Angels. Jesus replied to the crowd and said this voice you heard was for you and not for me. There were two opinions of the crowd, but both agreed that they heard a sound.

We can all agree that God is a spirit, and he is the source of the sound and voice these people hear. To better understand what's being heard, you must get closer to the source, which is a spirit-to-spirit connection. I like to say we live in times where we must learn in reversal, which means what broke our connection in the first place. If God can talk, then why can't I hear him. He lives and speaks from the spiritual realm, but we live in the natural world. Listening to him requires listening to spiritual words - His word and understanding His tone of voice. For example, our cellphones vibrate in a silent mode, but you still can hear and feel it. I repeat, "it's in a 'silent mode' that you can hear and feel". It's loudest when it's stillness around you. Imagine it is 2:45 a.m., the room is quiet, and you're sound asleep. Suddenly, the phone vibrates and rattles to the floor. That silent mode can still wake you up. The vibration could have been a ringing or text message.

On a normal night, thoughts of an emergency may run through your head. Maybe your spouse's thought is, "Well, who is that?!" Adam in Genesis had a similar situation with his spouse. It was an emergency and a "who is it?" at that moment. Adam's intimacy was broken when he and his wife were deceived and sinned against God's commandments. The guilt and shame of it made them cover themselves up. Genesis 3:8-10 says, "In the evening, there was a nice cool wind. The Lord God walked in the garden. The man and the woman heard the sound of the Lord God. They hid themselves behind some trees so that God would not see them. The man replied, 'I heard you in the garden. I was afraid because I had no clothes, so I hid myself from you.'" Adam had no noise of cars or electronics surrounding him. There was no radios or TV in their presence. In the cool of the wind were peace and quietness. Imagine you're in a large garden working naked, and suddenly, you hear the crackling of footsteps pressing through the grass. Your thoughts sense the fear of judgement which causes you to run for cover. They ran and hid themselves because they were alarmed by a sound. They were sensitive to the vibration of God pressing towards them. Because of sin, Adam and Eve were now aware and dominated by their natural senses instead of their spiritual senses. They were now practically living on a spiritual death row and were now sensing judgement coming their way.

As a new believer, I learned three important clues from this passage of scripture. The first thing is to start to pay attention to your thoughts and feelings. You have your own garden of life that you work inside of, and it's your mind. You also had an enemy in that garden who was deceiving you with lies and caused you to sin. If you are going about your life and you start to sense some fear of judgement all of a sudden, become aware. I've accepted Christ and made my confession to him, and I started to notice I'm having thoughts of death for some reason. Why am I going to church, coming home trying to live righteously, and I'm thinking about this? Fearful thoughts are just your mind's way of protecting you from any danger by asking questions like, "What is this?" If you don't see anything dangerous around you and you're starting to have these thoughts, the better question to ask inside is, "Who is this"? This question leads me to the second clue: the quietness of the natural.

In other words, we live in a world of distractions, and everything is calling for our attention. There are lots of noise around us all day, and we must take time away from them. Taking time away from what we hear, see, touch and taste. Getting in tune with the spiritual senses is denying the gratifications of what your flesh wants. And the third clue is - the renewing of your mind. This clue is important because once you accept Christ, your spirit is saved, not your body.

Think of it this way, your garden is your mind, and you were working in it all your life doing things you wanted to. As I said, we must live and learn in reversal. So, we lived in fear, shame, and guilt because of sin. We grew to live in separation from God and not recognizing Him or believing He exists. We renew the mind because it only learns natural things, and spiritual things don't make sense. You may be having fearful thoughts because you now have the spirit of God living inside you, and he is sensing his presence drawing near to you. Your natural mind can't see it, but your spiritual senses are picking it up - causing confusion and fear. Fear is a natural response because the body only dies, but spirits don't. Death is only a separation, and you are now hearing and feeling the vibration from God calling you to separate from the old way of thinking about the world. You are a spirit now, and you are alive to spiritual things. God wants you to know the truth. Renew the mind to know the truth, and the truth will set you free. Adam ran from God because he was vibing with God, but he separated himself from God with the desires of the flesh to sin. We separate ourselves from God because we vibe more with the world and our desires. Even though I was saved, I only recognized the church, but I didn't recognize God. I was like a deer in the woods, going about my days just eating and living as usual. And all of a sudden, I heard a crackle behind me. I look up and don't see anything. But now I'm sensing danger, so I run - running from the fear of being killed in my natural mind.

The sound of God is sensing his presence with your spirit. You get in His garden of words and start to listen to what He sounds like. If what you're hearing in the natural setting sounds like what you've heard or read in the Bible, then that's the sound of God. If what I just explained to you sounds like what you're going through, then that's the sound of God. He wants you to hear these stories or situations for a reason. He's trying to get your attention and become aware of him. He's basically drawing closer to you so you can draw closer to him. He wants you to understand him and the things of the spirit. In other words, he wants to vibe with you, and you vibe with him. Like kids, you may be hearing the vibrations of thunder, but you have nothing to fear because God doesn't give us the spirit of fear but love, power, and a sound mind.

CHAPTER THREE
A Familiar Voice

In the deep of the night hours, it's quiet in the house. It's pitch-black dark, no fan blades are spinning, no TVs are on, and everyone is sound asleep, including me. Suddenly, I hear my sister call me "SHERWIN", and my eyes immediately open. I thought nothing of it and dozed back off to sleep. The next night, the same situation applies, everything is quiet, and I'm sound asleep. "SHERWIN"! I opened my eyes but stood up this time. Now, I know I'm not tripping in my thoughts. My sister doesn't even live with me, but I keep hearing her voice for some reason. This incident happened again two nights later, and I was starting to get a little worried. I approached my pastor and mentioned that I was hearing my name being called at night for some reason. I explained it's only happening when I'm sleeping. He paused for a minute, then instructed me when the next time I hear it respond with, "Speak Lord, your servant is listening." "Okay", I responded.

Have you ever been in an environment and in your thought, you heard someone calling your name? Think about your family gatherings, and it's about three or four conversations going on, the TV is on, and someone called you for your attention. Your response is determined by the voice calling, right? If it's your grandmother or mother, it's "Ma'am". A cousin might get a response of, "Huh". And a nagging brother or sister would get a "What?". Even if you weren't really paying attention, you still would know who was calling you because of the familiar voices around. But let's just say you're in a mixed crowd of unknown people, and someone calls out your name. It's going to get your attention because somebody knows you, but you are trying to figure out who is this. Now, these are scenarios of noise around you, but when it's quiet, it should be easy to recognize who's calling you, right? I would think so when we speak in the natural setting, but we get confused when it comes to God.

Samuel had a similar situation when God was trying to reach him. Samuel was a young man who ministered before the Lord in the tent meetings under the Priest Eli. In these times, the open visions of God were rare, but Samuel heard what he first believed to be Eli calling him during the night. Even though Samuel was serving in the Tabernacle, he still didn't know God, and the word of the Lord had not been revealed to him (1 Samuel 3:7). The first three times God called Samuel, he responded to Eli. However, Eli understood what was happening and instructed him to respond thus, "Speak Lord, for your servant is listening." As you can see, Samuel responded to the familiar voice that was closed to him. I heard the voice of my close relative, but the voice came in silence. I probably would've run to my sister as well had she been in the same house, but this is a lesson learned that God voice can sound familiar.

The scripture says, "For God speaketh once, yea twice, but man perceiveth it not" (Job 33:14). There are many voices in the land, but which one is God's voice? This scripture of passages teaches us that God speaks to get your attention. And he does it more than once, but we have a hard time recognizing it. It's a few examples I want you to think about when it comes to recognizing his voice. The first is with newborns. Babies spend nine months developing inside and hearing the voice of their mother. At birth, their senses can tell when

Mama is around. If she lays the baby on her chest, he can sense that food is nearby, latching on the breast. The mother and newborn have a close bond from the beginning. But the baby came from the father. The father could've been speaking to the belly the whole time, but the child was inside another world. His origin was from his father, but he wouldn't recognize his voice when he was born. The father can speak once and twice, but he still won't know who he is. Babies perceive daddy's voice by what they constantly hear and see from him. It's a relationship that must be built with time.

The whole time you've been in your own world, God was speaking good things about you. He said things like, "I love you, and I can't wait until you're born in the Spirit so I can watch you grow. I promise I will provide and protect you from anything harmful to you. I know you're clingy to what's familiar, but I'm always here". Babies feel protected by their mothers but must learn to trust this other man that's around, which is his father. He learns the father voice by how he talks every day. This point brings me to another example: The way you talk can be heard through a text message. Have you ever heard anyone say, "you text how you talk?" If you've been around someone for a while, you're familiar with the words they use in conversations. Have you ever had someone play on your phone? Meaning you get a text message from an odd number, but the text message sounds like the voice of a person you've dealt with before? They tried to disguise themselves by a different number, but their voice was still heard through their words. Voices can sound so familiar that it travels through people. In other words, you can meet someone by their voice before you meet them physically. For example, I met my father n law before I met him physically. I could hear his voice through my wife and could tell exactly who he was. Because they had a close bond, I knew some things she spoke out of her mouth came from him. I recognized how he thinks, by how she talks, which we've learned in scripture as a man thinketh so is he.

With God, it's no different. You see, the way you think is the way you speak, and the way God thinks is the way God speaks. God said, "let this mind be in you as it is in Christ". "My thoughts are not your thoughts". Thoughts are just words concealed, and you can hear them in your own mind. Right now, you should be able to tell what I sound like through the words I'm writing to you. You can tell a bit about my life and who I really am by reading. I'm basically feeding you with my thoughts so you can know me. If I quote something from this book on social media or hear my voice speak somewhere, you may recognize me by what I'm saying. For God speak once and twice, but man can't perceive it because man doesn't have knowledge of God. Knowledge comes from reading and studying thoughts. Samuel didn't recognize God's voice because Samuel didn't know God. Similarly, babies don't recognize the father's voice because the babies don't know the father. I didn't recognize the voice speaking because I didn't have knowledge of God speaking. It isn't until someone opens their mouth that you know who they are. You could see me in public and judge me based on my appearance, but you will never know who I really am if I never open my mouth.

God's voice not only sounds familiar, but it's quiet. 1 King 19:12 says, "God spoke in a still small voice". Elijah was on the run, and God quietly spoke to him. He told him to stand on the mountain and wait until I passed in front of him. Strong winds broke the rocks of the mountain, an earthquake occurred, a fire blazed, and God was in none of these things. After these things passed, Elijah heard the still small voice speaking. God basically whispered in his ear and asked him what is he doing here, running, and hiding? My focus is not the natural things around, which God can use to get your attention; it's the whisper in the ear. If someone whispers in your hearing, that means they're close to you. Most men won't let another man whisper in their ear. You are talking about a man law violation. The reaction proves that "Hey man, you to close, back up a lil bit and just talk to me man to man." But this shows how close God was to Elijah, and it shows how close God is to you.

God doesn't want to use natural disasters just to get you. He wants you to know he's so close to you that you may feel violated. "I see the things you do, and I'm watching you run and hide from your problems. Yes, I'm all in your business, but I'm concerned about you". This whispering represents that closeness but also secrets. If you want to hear a secret from someone, they can whisper it in your ear. God knows all about your secrets. Meaning the ones you know about and those you don't know about. You know the things you did in private that you're not proud of, God forgives you. But God whispers to inform you of things you could do that you haven't yet. You have secret potentials, and God is the only one that knows it. More knowledge of Him means more knowledge of yourself.

To hear the voice of God, you must listen with the inner ear. The voice I heard came from the inner ear. The inner ear is the heart of man. Look at it this way; the word "ear" is located in the middle of the word "heart" - hEARt. Your inner ear is within your heart. God speaks to the heart, not the mind. This is the problem with the whole world, it's the things in our heart, and that's where God wants to get reach. One of my favorite scriptures is Proverb 4:23, "Guard your heart with all diligence; from out of it are the issues of life"". Every issue you struggle with comes from your heart. You're only familiar with things or people that your heart is familiar with. The heart has a voice, and you can hear it through the mouth. When the mouth speaks, it's usually the heart talking. God's voice sounds familiar when He is speaking about something in your heart.

Have you ever been in church, and it seemed like the pastor is preaching about something you're dealing with in your life? He doesn't even know you but is talking about your secrets. That burning feeling in your heart is God speaking. God is having a heart-to-heart with you. This is God's way of speaking through his word, through a person, and to your heart. This is the power of the Spirit moving. If you understand this, then you're learning how to recognize God voice through the heart, through people and his word. His primary way of speaking to your heart is through his words. The Gospel of Luke 24:31-32 says, "Their eyes became clear, and they recognized him. But then he disappeared, and they could no longer see him. They said to each other, "When he talked to us, it was like fire that was burning inside us. We felt it while we were walking along the road. We also felt it when he was explaining God's message in the Bible". Jesus rose from death and was making his appearance around town. Jesus had a glorified body, but no one recognized him. They only recognized him because he did and said familiar things before he died on the cross. God can speak to you throughout the day. You are walking along the road in your everyday life when He is talking. It's not only in a church building.

The familiar voice is a quiet voice that's close by you all the time. It's within the heart, and listening to it is the hardest when so much attention gets to the minds. Samuel had his day-to-day routines in the Tabernacle, so God spoke to him when it was silent. Elijah was running from the things going on with his life, so God whispered after the commotions. So, God is speaking to you once and twice, but you don't perceive it with the mind, its quietly with the heart...

CHAPTER FOUR
Visitations Are Closed

There I was, stomach full of eating sonics coney dogs, my body relaxed from a hot shower, the sound of the A/C blowing a cool breeze in the room, and I finally drifted off to sleep. Suddenly, something appeared to me out of nowhere before my eyes as the night went on. This thing had the appearance of Jell-O. But it was thick and clear. This is the best way I can describe what I saw, but this appearance covered my eyes. I couldn't breathe, and it was complete silence around me. I heard a voice speak to me and ask, "Do you want to see on the other side?". For some strange reason, I responded, "Yes". And immediately, what I was seeing vanished from my eyes. With my head still on the pillow, my eyes were wide open and wondering what in the world had just happened! It's quiet in the room, and my wife and children are sound asleep. About ten seconds later, I jumped up out the bed, yelling: "I'm going to die!" My heart was racing, and my flight system was kicked in immediately. I yelled at my wife to get up and take me to the hospital and ran towards the bathroom. With my legs trembling, I tried to use the bathroom, but I ended up slamming the seat down. I turned on the shower and just ran out of the bathroom to grab my shoes. We were inside a hotel room, and I started turning on all the lights, looking for my shoes. It was about 2 a.m., and my wife was asking what was going on with me. All I kept saying was, "I'm dying, I'm dying". She immediately came towards me and held me in prayer. Prayer wasn't working at this moment because I was still in a state of shock. I rushed out of the room, slammed the door behind me and walked around the building, gasping for deep breaths. As much noise I was making that night, the whole world was sleeping. My kids never woke up, and nobody was in and out of the hotel rooms. It's usually noisy traffic from the intersection by the hotel, but nothing was moving that night.

I remember those days when we had antennas attached to our televisions. If we were experiencing any static on the screen, it was usually an interference problem or a connection problem. The antennas had to be sitting in the right position for the picture to show up clear. Imagine you sleeping at night, and someone turns on the T.V. and it wakes you up out your sleep. The same metaphor applies to God. You can be connected to God in your spirit but still have an interference. I accepted Christ, but I wasn't reading His words. The distractions from the outside world interfered with me from knowing what was in the Bible. I didn't know what I experienced was in the Bible. So, God had to come and shift my antennas. I now sit in the right location and can show you in Job 4:12-16 reads, "Now a thing was secretly brought to me, and my ear received a little thereof. In thoughts from the visions of the night, when deep sleep falleth on men, Fear and trembling, which made all my bones to shake. Then a spirit passed before my face; the hair of my flesh stood up: It stood still, but I could not discern the form thereof: An image was before my eyes, there was silence, and I heard a voice, saying..." It's proven that we fall asleep in stages, but we also wake up in stages. Spiritually speaking, we experience stages of awakenings. This was the beginning and my first visitation from heaven.

"Hear now my words: If there is a prophet among you, I, the Lord, will show myself to him in a vision, and I will speak to him in a dream", Number 12:6. Prophets in the Bible had the role of being the middleman between God and man. Most of the prophets showed up on the scene with warnings or reminders from God. Some of these prophets were called seers because their ministry was primarily on what they could see. They were able to hear audible voices from God and see things in the spiritual realms. You may be a prophet or seer but not aware of it. Some things in your life may be interfering with your reception of things from God. One of the five-fold ministry gifts is a prophet. If you're holding that gift, it may be time for God to cut on your T.V. at night to wake you up. When God gives visions, they can be seen opened and closed. A vision is something you see with your spiritual eyes. An open vision is when God opens your eyes to see things in the spirit while you're conscious and awake. The closed visions are things we see while we're asleep, and the eyes are closed. To me, there are different levels of faith to see visions. Based on my experiences, I believe closed visions happen before open visions. I say that because this first visit freaked me out when I was asleep, so trying to handle things with an open eye may be terrifying. I guess you can say we watch too many movies and T.V. In the Old Testament days, God had to reveal himself through prophets because they didn't have a finished Bible. If God chose anyone, they recorded the things they've experienced, and what God spoke so we would have a reference today.

At the beginning of any relationship, both individuals must introduce themselves. Since God already knows you, your chances of knowing him may only come when the visitation hours are closed. In other words, he can't connect with you during the day because your life has too many interferences. Job 33:15-16 reads, "In a dream, in a vision of the night, when deep sleep falleth upon men, in slumbering upon the bed; then he openeth the ears of men, and sealeth their instruction". These verses are for our reference that God can speak to you through your dreams. He does it sometimes because your mind is so preoccupied during the day that you might miss his instructions or warnings. If you start to have strange dreams at night, start to pay attention. This may be God's way of introducing himself to you. When God wants a relationship with you, pay attention to how he speaks to you consistently.

Before this revelation, I noticed that I was having strange dreams suddenly. It started to flow every night. It's important to write down what you see in these dreams. Because we sleep in stages, God usually speaks just before we wake up for the day. He does it so you won't forget the dream's details and it's fresh on your mind. I learned that it's important to guard what you're seeing and hearing through the day because it interferes with the mind at night. That's important for you, who holds the office of the two prophets. One prophet's job is to hear primarily; the Seer prophets primarily sees. Seers are highly sensitive to spirits and can hear and see in this realm. Your eyes are a gift to specialize in this ministry.

What I'm saying is, we learned from our experiences with God. Jeremiah, the prophet, was a seer. God give him eye exams to test him on his visions. The things you see at night in visions could be a test for your eyes. God is preparing you before he sends you out on your mission. You write down what you see from the picture God gives you, and he tests your vision's accuracy. Think of yourself as an eagle in training. You first learn about the teacher, learn who you are, and learn what you can do. Let me share some of the things I've learned and experienced in night school training. The first thing God showed me was death and being in the presence of Hell. God showed me what I deserved, but I'm saved because of His mercy and grace by believing in Christ. Death was a dream, but Hell was a vision. I saw myself underground and taken off all my clothes in the dream. I was standing beside an open casket, and a few other caskets were around. It seemed like I was about to get inside, but I woke up immediately. The very next night, I was in the presence of

Hell. Hell is real, you all. I didn't see fire but where I was standing inside seemed like an upstairs lobby of a jailhouse, but all the guardrails and posts were in Gold.

God specifically showed me the steam that was constantly blowing on the rails, and I felt it. Think of a Sauna, and you will get the picture. (FYI: God doesn't send you to Hell, you CHOOSE to go). That's why he said, choose life! But let's move on. I hate to talk about this, but God showed me visions of the death of other people. We went through a tough season of members passing away within my church family. This was a time of testing my eyes. I say that because I saw two of them clearly but didn't know what to do about it. One of them stood in front of the church teaching as usual and fell out on the floor. She never regained consciousness and eventually passed away days later. It wasn't her face I saw in the vision, but the body was teaching in Sunday school. Everyone got up to lay hands on her head, but she fell and was snoring on the floor. I said it's important to write these things down in detail because the vision and reality happened in the same spot she was standing. I held on to this guilt feeling because I believed we were supposed to lay hands on her head and pray for her before this ever happened. God bless her soul. Still, we laid hands on her head in the vision because she passed from a brain aneurysm.

In the other vision, I saw her face clearly laying in a casket. I held on to this for some weeks, but finally, I had the courage to tell her what I saw. I tried to sugarcoat it while explaining, but she told me to obey God by telling everything in detail. The next week she approached me and said that she and God were on the same page and thanked me for it. She never told me what the issue was, and I really didn't want to hear about it. I thought that the dream meant something spiritual, and we could move on. Well, I was wrong. That was a literal dream that happened a month later. God bless her soul as well. But before she passed away, I visited her in the hospital. As soon as I opened the door, she looked the same way as she did in the vision. Her hair was the same. Her eyes looked the same, and her lips were the exact shade of color, just like the vision. Whatever was going on with her and God, I knew this was probably the last time I would see her.

Whoever said this ministry is easy is a liar. So, you know, real prophets come with warnings and things ahead of time that are serious. I'm speaking with aggression because all these Oprah prophets out here are deceiving people with prosperity and blessing prophecies. You get a car, and you get a car, and you get a house prophecy pass out. Yes, God is in the blessing business, but he cares about your SOUL first. Don't get this twisted; God is serious!! I secretly cried many nights knowing that I saw these things coming, but this was all part of the training. I also experienced the presence of Angels and Demons. The face of a demon and spirits, and hearing their voices. The verse says God open the ear. Well, he opened my ear to hear a glimpse of what was going on. At night there was a lot of activity going on while we were asleep. Angelic spirits are real and speak just like we do. One night, an Angel brought me a personal message: "Not yet prison, you will fall". These were the exact words I heard. Though it didn't make sense to me, God confirmed it later. The message was for me, but I also realized how fast these spirits move. Think of a fighter jet blowing past you, and you hear the effects of the wind behind it. God opened my ear; I heard a lot of talking in the background, and here comes this rush of wind approaching my ears with these words and then rushing away. And just take note, when God or His Angels come in your presence, you will feel an overwhelming peace around you. I prayed many nights for Him to come around again. He did but didn't say anything. I just recognized the presence.

These are just some of the things I've experienced. To share a little of what I have learned and seen so far. The more you stay plugged into God, the clearer your visions will be. John was in the Isle that is called Patmos, and he was the one that God told to write what he saw. He wrote the Book of Revelations about everything he saw in the spirit. He was blessed to see heaven and describe it the best way possible to what he witnessed. He had visions of the end times and saw what some would go through before Christ returned. Im writing for the same reason, and I know I'm not the only one who witness similar things. I'm just a remote being used to turn your channel to God and want you to become aware of these spiritual realities. The right connections help you to see things clearly on the screen, but sometimes God wants us to watch T.V. at night. The Bible explains how some people saw Angels in open visions of the day. I tried to search for them myself, but God informed me to stop looking for them. He said when the time comes, you will see them but move on with your journey. I say that because, again, I believe its levels to our faith. The first level may be to pass night school when the visitation hours are closed. Remember that and Stay Blessed...

CHAPTER FIVE

What's In Your Hands

Then Moses answered the Lord and said, "What if they will not believe me or take seriously what I say? For they may say, 'The Lord has not appeared to you.' And the Lord said to him, "What is that in your hand? (Exodus 4:1-2). How hard is it to get others to believe what God told you or, in my case, what he showed me? It's easy to get caught up in what others think rather than believing in what you think. Studies show that people's biggest fear is public speaking. It's the biggest because we value other people opinions more than our own.

We worry about how we look and sound in the public eyes and dread the responses. Confidence, to me, is knowing and trusting what you believe. God appeared to Moses in a burning bush and commissioned him to go back to Egypt to confront the king and lead the people to the promised land. Moses had a lack of confidence because of his own flaws. Moses knew some things about himself, and God knew some things about him. As you read the rest of that chapter, God disregarded every excuse Moses was trying to give. Instead, he pointed Moses to this first sign and told him to use this to show proof of His word. The appearance of God made me feel the same as Moses. I wanted to show proof of what miraculous sign God showed me in my life. I held on to this for a while because, in my heart, I said, "What if they will not believe me or take seriously what I say? What if they don't believe you were around me, and I can't do what you told me to do?" God's response again, "What is that in your hands?" God wants us to have confidence in him and what we already have in our hands.

In this season of my life, I was receiving a lot of revelations from God and myself. But to me, he was starting to get a little quiet or at least I thought he was, and I prayed a simple prayer in my heart. I said, "Lord, you are kind of quiet, and I'm not seeing much of your hands moving around me. Please, give me a sign or something to show yourself if you're still around. I know I'm not supposed to be asking for signs all the time but do something where I won't miss you, and it's in my face." So, the following day, I got myself together for work as usual and left outside the house. My vehicle was parked in my backyard, and I walked to open my door and sat inside to crank it up and immediately, my jaws dropped. I froze for about three minutes, trying to take in what I was seeing. All kind of thoughts was running through my mind on who could've done this. I knew nobody came to my backyard and just drew this on my windshield. It's too cold outside for anybody to play games like that, and the light is just dawning. And who sketch something that perfect. You can't draw something that perfect for the first time without messing up and starting over in the same spot. But I remembered my prayer the day before. What was in my hands at that time is what's in everybody's hands all the time now. My trusted Phone! I had to take a snapshot of this and meditate on it all day. I was mad that I had to turn on my wiper because it would erase the image. I praised God all the way to work and tried to imagine how

He even did this. I said to myself, "God, you just did this before I walked out of the door, isn't it? You did this slickly, and I should've run to the back of the house just to try and catch you." (Laugh out loud).

Still in awe, I immediately shared this experience with my wife when I got to work. To me, her response was no real surprise at all. She knew God does supernatural things like this, but I didn't. At least, not in my life, but I was excited. She did ask an important question, though, "What does it mean?" I started reflecting within myself, "Hmmm, what does this mean for real? God, you could've drawn my name, or maybe, a cross, but why a basketball?" One thing I learned about God is that He says something or does anything that matches somewhere in His word. His word is literal, and His principles are applied in life situations. And to trace him, you must trace His word. So, I knew two places where this Miracle looked like something God does to try and understand its meaning. The first place is in Daniel, Chapter 5, where God wrote on the wall.

In short story form, King Belshazzar was the ruler of Babylon and was full of pride by praising the gods of gold, silver, bronze, iron, wood, and stone. One night the king held a feast in a banquet hall with his household and a thousand of his noblemen. As they carried on worshipping their idol gods and getting wasted, God sent him a sign. A human hand appeared near them and wrote him a devastating message in a language no one could understand. Being frightened to death, the king panicked and offered a bribe that anyone who could interpret this message would be crowned in gold and purple. No one could interpret it but Daniel. The message God sent was for his destruction that very night.

The point I want to make is that God sees all and knows all. This was a personal message just for the king. God knew him and saw what was in his heart the whole time he ruled. Daniel also knew what it meant, and he also knew God. He knew God was about to deal with him, and he denied the prideful bribe and interpreted the message, anyway. God sees something in your heart that will remind you of yourself. Imagine losing a loved one that was close to your heart, and you've seen a sign or something that reminded you of them. In my late childhood, anybody close to me knew that I was married to basketball. I held hands with the ball every chance I could get, and that was a game I fell in love with it. We divorced for reconcilable differences, but part of my heart developed a small hole. Well, God knows us just like close friends may know us and see what's closest to you in your heart. Because I asked God to show me His hand, He decided to draw my heart for me. I realized then that

He knew me and knew about a deep feeling inside by answering the prayer.

By this happening in the morning's dew, the second place was in the Book of Judges, chapter 6. In this chapter, a man named Gideon was a mighty warrior according to the Angel of the Lord (Judges 6:12). He was the leader who was commissioned to lead Israel in battle and received victory by the grace of God. For seven years, the Israelites faced invasions from the Midianites, Amalekites, and Eastern foreigners who ruined their crops and destroyed their cattle. Because they felt overpowered and outnumbered, Gideon was afraid and hid from the Midianites. But God heard the prayers of the Israelites and commissioned Gideon to go into battle and rescue Israel. Gideon wasn't sure of himself and the calling. He needed reassurance.

In other words, Gideon asked for signs of confirmation. Judge 6:36-39, "Then Gideon said to God, 'If you're going to rescue Israel through me, as you have spoken, behold, I will put a fleece of wool on the threshing floor. If there is dew only on the fleece, and it is dry on all the ground, then I will know that you will rescue Israel through me as you've said.' And it was so. When he got up early the next morning and squeezed the dew out of the fleece, he wrung from it a bowl full of water. Then Gideon said to God, 'Do not let your anger burn against me so that I may speak once more. Please let me make a test once more with the fleece; now let the fleece be dry and let there be dew on all the ground'."

As you can see, Gideon prayed for confirmation twice and received his answer the very next morning. God knew what was in Gideon's heart and answered his prayer exactly so he wouldn't miss him. I knew better not to test God, but I needed reassurance like Gideon. I want to point out why Gideon was hesitant of asking God for a sign. As we know, some people in this world must use sign language to communicate. God can speak in any language, but sign language is something he would rather not do. God wants you to have faith that pleases him. He's a speaking God and wants you to believe he talks back to you. To God, asking for signs all the time shows your lack of belief in him. Like Gideon, if he told you who you will become, do you need a sign to confirm? Or, like me, if he promised, "I'll never abandon you or forsake you", do you need a sign? I'm not saying God won't respond with confirmations; he did it twice with Gideon. Even though I'm writing about it now, some still won't believe it. Jesus already spoke it in his word, John 4:48, "Unless you people see signs and wonders", Jesus told him, "You will never believe."

This miracle sign proves that God has hands to write and knows a lot about you. But there are some things about you that you don't know. I knew I had a love for basketball in me the whole time, but I didn't know I had the ability to write and speak. Gideon didn't know he was a mighty warrior who would lead his people to a battle victory. Because he was in hiding, his leadership quality was hidden the whole time. It took a message from God to see himself differently. You may not be hiding physically, but something else in you is hidden. You are focused on how you're outnumbered, on other people's success in life, and you don't feel adequate for anything beyond you're 9 to 5. Like Gideon, and like Moses, God is saying, "What is that in your hand?" What's in your hand represents what your potential is. What else do you see? Let me put it to you this way, you were created in the Image of God. And God has the whole world in His hand. God is the Creator - an inventor, a carpenter, a speaker, a writer, a prophet, a fighter, a teacher, a designer, a father, a leader, an entrepreneur! God has power - he's a healer, deliverer, provider. God is everything! And because He created you, you have the capabilities to do something He did. God is saying it's something I did, that you can do! I thought I lost a part of me that I loved, but that sign was to point me in the direction of something deeper inside. What you lost may be painful, but there may be some purposes behind it. God's word is already written, and he has written something about you that you can do. The problem is you're searching in the wrong places. Moses excuses were everywhere else but what he possessed. Gideon's focus was on everybody else but himself. Moses was a writer and leader like God. He wrote the Ten Commandments and led people from Egypt to the promised land. Gideon was a leader and fighter like God.

I am now becoming a writer and leader like God because I'm sharing my story and leading you towards Him. What is in my hands may not look like what is in your hands. So, don't focus on that. God is trying to shift your focus on yourself because there is something about you that is unique. The Bible is full of stories about different people's lives. And if you can just get it in your hands, you may find yourself inside. In other words, where you are in life currently is somewhere inside the Bible. You just must find it. Your lack of confidence is how you see yourself, but God sees you differently. He sees Himself when He looks at you, and He wants you to believe that. What is in your hands is your potential, and it is meant to empower and lead others...

CHAPTER SIX
Call It In The Air

When we hear that God calls someone, the typical thinking is a calling to become a pastor or someone standing in a pulpit. Standing in a pulpit preaching and teaching a crowd of people is the usual idea of what we think God has in mind. I used to think that way too, but I've grown to see God better than that. As we see today, pulpits in churches have become stages in what we call some mega-churches now. There are a lot of wolves in sheep clothing, pretending to care for the flock. But deep inside, they're probably doing it all for the money and fame. So, some believers may see the mega's as a problem. But Jesus said we can judge the tree by the fruits it bears. And just because we have a lot of ministers on stages now doesn't mean they're all ministering for money. Sometimes God calls people to different stages in the secular world as well. I want to clear up some static in your mind if you're trying to see things differently with God regarding callings, stages, money, and fame.

One of the biggest stages in life I see is sports especially, at a professional level. For example, American football is played by two teams on a field with goal lines on each end. You have one team on offence and the other one on defense. The offensive job is to outscore the other by advancing the ball down the field. The defensive job is to stop the advancement and take control of the ball. You can't put up points unless you have the ball in your hands, and you protect it enough to move down the field. This ball represents the dream because both teams are after it, which is the goal. There are two sides but one goal - get the ball in your hands. I've heard many stories where an athlete said my father put the ball in my hands at a young age, and the rest was history. Let this sink in, a father places a rubber ball in his son's hands at three years old, and 20 years later, that ball made him millions. Would I say a dream come true right? But where did the dream originate from - the father or the son? At three years old, that child doesn't understand the stage of that dream. All he sees is a ball in his hand and what he sees on T.V. What's the odds of him making it to the pros? My answer is that the longer he can believe the dream that was put in his hands, the better the odds of him winning. But in between a dream and reality is a process of understanding rules, laws, and developments. What exactly is a dream? And what is reality, anyway? What are the odds of believing in a dream long enough vs believing in reality? I guess you can say that's a game of life, right? What side are you attacking for, and what side are you defending?

At the beginning of the Book of Daniel, Chapter 1, Daniel served in the royal courts of King Nebuchadnezzar. Nebuchadnezzar, King of Babylon, took over Jerusalem and wanted to draft young noblemen of Israel to his team. Daniel was a strong, fit, handsome young man. And God gifted him in knowledge and skills in literature and wisdom. Daniel also had the ability in understanding visions and dreams. All the men in Israel went into training for three years to learn the ways of Babylonians. Let's just say this was collegiate years before making it to the professional levels. At the end of three years, it was time for them to be presented in front of the king. Daniel and his friends' appearances were healthier than any other players in the combined training for ten days because they refused to give up their diet of water and veggies. That's a quick note that we can learn from Daniel - the healthier you eat, the healthier you look and feel. Finally, Daniel and his friends were all drafted and began to serve next to the king and rulers of the land. If you read the whole Book of Daniel, you will see how he had favor with the secular world because of his faithfulness to God. He used and understood his giftings, and he continued to draw strength in prayer when faced with difficulties.

Daniel had one difficulty concerning a dream he had about a future event. Even though he saw it in a dream, it was a future reality. So, he needed understanding and prayed for it. Some of us may need to understand a dream we may be seeing inside of us because it may be connected to our purpose - even if the dream seems secular.

Your dream and reality must meet in the middle. The middle is what I like to call your starting point. Before you try to reach any dreams inside you, you must recognize where you are in your chosen career or field. Start where you are and reflect on the motives behind your desire. Where did this dream even come from? As a young man, seeing athletes from the outside looking in made me desire what they had in life. Before every football game, there is a meeting in the middle of the field. The team captains and the referee meet for a coin toss. The referee tosses it up and says, "Call it in the air!" This coin has two sides, and it's a representation of money.

I hear many people say money is the root of all evil. I hear it in rap lyrics, on the radio, and some quote it on social meetings. Many people are starting to believe this, and I'll be the first to say it's a lie. They think they're quoting the Bible verse, but the Bible didn't say that. 1 Timothy 6:10 reads, "For the LOVE of money is a root of all kinds of evil. It is through this craving that some have wandered away from the faith and pierced themselves with many pangs." What you love is the motive behind any means necessary which births some evil things we see. Some desires may be coveting what someone else has, which is a sin. So, it's not a problem to have money, but it's a problem when money controls you. Money is neutral and has two sides to it, like the coin. You can use the money for good or evil purposes. You can earn money from working 8 hours on a job, or you can steal it from the bank. You can be paid for transporting people, or you can be paid for killing people. You can see money as your obligation to pay tithe in honoring God, or you can see money as paying for your pastor Rolls Royce. It's always two sides. The same is true when it comes to your field of career. You may think your calling or purpose is outside of your job, but it's two sides of the coin.

Let us look at it in another way. Jesus was the master of using natural things for spiritual purposes. Peter was a businessman in the fishing industry. Jesus told him, "Follow me, and I will make you fishers of men." In other words, whatever you're good at, God will use you to attract people. For example, we all know we must pay taxes. God doesn't exempt us from paying for our obligations in the economy. In Matthew 17:25-27, Jesus asked Peter if they were exempted from paying taxes. Peter responded, no. Then Jesus told him to go to the sea and cast a hook, take the first fish that comes up, open his mouth, and you will find a coin to pay for the both of us. This text is powerful because it teaches natural and spiritual principles. The point I want to get across is that you may be after something that provides a need or a want naturally, but God is using natural things for spiritual purposes. Peter was after the coin; Jesus was after the fish. Remember Jesus said, "I will make you fishers of men." So, this fish represents people, and you can only catch a fish by the bait you provide. God knows who has what you're looking for, and he is using your expertise, talents, gifts, and abilities to get them. You're after the money; God is after the soul. Do you see the two sides of the coin?

The money causes us to look up in the air like watching the coin tossed. The money also causes us to look for different careers and jobs that pay well. There are a lot of natural careers that can literally put us in the air, like working for NASA or in the Aviation field. Some of us may dream of going out of space or becoming pilots, but that's not the only career that would get us in the air. You may want to produce movies or host your own talk show or podcast. You may want to become a singer or rap artist. You may have a desire to run for mayor in your city or become the next president of your country. The career fields of film, music, government and politics, and sports all have careers in high places. This is the other side to look at it because it's in high places spiritually. When you think of a pilot flying a plane, you think of naturally transporting people in the air. These other careers are spiritual because it gets the attention of a lot of people. As I said, God uses natural things for spiritual purposes, but spiritual things have two sides as well. Satan uses natural things for evil purposes.

If you haven't read Ephesians 6:12, "For we wrestle not against flesh and blood, but against principalities, against rulers, against powers and rulers of the darkness of this world, against spiritual wickedness in High Places." The high places are the airwaves of radio, T.V., and the media. Any advertisements or anything that gets the attention to control people's minds. The high places are the high positions that influence the people the most. We all watch movies; we all listen to radio and podcasts. The world as we know it now revolves around social media. My question to you is, "If you're in one of these high positions, what messages are you giving off to the people that are watching?" Before takeoff, a pilot speaks through the intercom and prepares the audience with a message before they fly. You usually don't see him, but you do hear his voice. Before you reach high levels in life, check the message of your voice, and match it with the word of God. How does your body language speak to other people in the field you're pursuing? Check the attitude of your voice before you start that podcast.

Are you showing violence and half-naked women walking around in your music videos? In your movies, are you showing fornications and homosexuality? If you're slacking at a job now with laziness and just getting by, what do you expect if your business gets in the air? If you desire to become a mayor, then what are the motives behind your speeches? Are you really for the people? When you vote, are you only voting for popularity or principles? Spirits operate in high places, and spirits work by law if you don't know. So, the minute you vote a law in or out, you've just invited a spirit to operate in that place.

It's a fight in the air, and you're called to it. Daniel prayed for understanding, and his answer came but was delayed. God heard Daniel's prayer and immediately dispatched an angel to deliver the message to understand his dream. The angel was delayed because of the fight with evil spirits in the heavenly realms. You may be praying for some understanding in your life but just know your answer is on the way. I've experienced this fight in the supernatural realm. I can look back now and explain exactly what was happening to me in the spirit. When God decided to call me, I was confused about the purpose of the calling. The signs were all around me, but I couldn't see them. The week came around for our church revival, and we had different pastors preaching every night at 7 pm. It seemed like in the mornings, I wake up and go to work just fine. But around 3'o clock is when the fight began. I started noticing a pattern from Monday to Friday around 3'o clock until I arrived at church service.

This intense anxiety and fear took over me. For the first two days, I kept it to myself because I was thinking maybe I needed to stop drinking energy drinks or get some more sleep. I was just thinking in the natural realm. But by Wednesday, it started getting worse, and I started to fear driving to work. I usually drive about 75 mph, but I was now driving 35 mph on the interstate road because I feared crashing and thoughts of killing myself. Something was happening to me, and I was in a state of confusion. I tried praying against it the best way I knew, but no answers. I called a friend of mine who I knew was more advanced in this spiritual realm, and he was the one who recognized the patterns. He told me this was a matter of life and death, and the enemy was trying to stop me from hearing a certain message from God. This started to make a little sense now because the time of the fight was on point. I really was fighting to go to church for the rest of that week, but I was determined to see if all this was true. Well, Friday came around, and we had a speaker who came from up North to deliver her word. I made sure I sat in the back so that I could deal with my anxiety and overwhelming feelings. She spoke about how she went through some traveling issues but was determined to make it to church. The spirit got my attention now because I related to that determination as well. She had a fight, and I was fighting too, but we both arrived. By the end of her sermon, she spoke a prophetic word. She confirmed everything I went through without even speaking to me directly. The very minute I received the word and God confirmed who I was, the fear and anxiety immediately left me.

The next week everything was back to normal, and I realized what the fight was all about. You see, there is always a fight in the air. And there are always two sides to the coin. You may be praying for answers and wonder why you haven't received what you're looking for. Your answer may be in a fight, but trust it's on the way. If you're going through a fight to reach something or to go somewhere, then just know you may be the answer to someone else prayers. The fight can come in all kinds of places to discourage you as well. If you received a word by faith from God and you start to hear other words that go against that, then that's a fight. If you are pursuing a dream and desire in your heart that's in agreement with God's word and people may start to discourage you, then that's a fight. The fight is not exempted in churches too. Some religious people can't see beyond the walls of the buildings and can make you feel guilty for pursuing secular dreams. You may hear you're just chasing money, but, in your reality, you're just chasing a dream. Some may call it chasing money, but God calls it IN THE AIR. God calls you in the air for a reason, and you're going somewhere.

CHAPTER SEVEN

Cut It Out

When it comes to the word "family", a few thoughts may run through your mind on its meaning. The immediate family normally includes a husband and wife with their children. A wider view may consist of grandparents, aunts, uncles, cousins and so on. Within the family usually demonstrates love, strength, and unity. Over time, the family bond becomes stronger. As we know, the holiday seasons are perfect for time to spend with our families. It's a time for traveling and visiting people you may not have seen throughout the year. Thanksgiving especially is a time for food preparations and your special family recipes to come forth. Everyone has that "Big Momma's House", where it's always one location where the whole family meets for dinner. The movie "Soul Food' is a good representation of this. You have 4 or 5 immediate families, all coming together in one location.

Some might say those were the good old days if that tradition had been broken. You know the days where it was laughter and jokes, the days of celebrating new editions to families and planning for future events and goals. The days of enjoying football games with beers and eating all day and night. Yeah, you know the familiar days when a lot of weight gain is going on. Yeah, that sounds like it could've been the good old days, but there are some bad old days as well. The bad old days are when people in families don't get along. We all know or may even experience some of these bad old days. The days when the family multiplied in numbers, but the numbers started dividing. The days when the atmosphere was love became an atmosphere of competition. The days of secret judgement because of my struggles or maybe, your sacrifices with life. I could go on and on, but you know exactly what I'm talking about. We can all agree to disagree to the point of blame, but something happened within the family that caused this shift from those days. The same thing that happened, or is happening, within your family is the same thing that happened in the first family. Let's break this down and see.

In Genesis Chapter 4, we see that Adam and Eve started their own family - man and wife with children. A simple role model of immediate family with nothing different from what we see now. In this story, I've learned that there are important roles to play in a family, and they are different jobs to do. I could tell Adam and Eve loved their children and raised them to know God. Adam and Eve taught their boys to work hard and do their best and taught them the way of life. Cain was the oldest, and he became a farmer and mastered the art of growing food. Abel, his younger brother, became a shepherd who raised and took care of the flock. As you can see, they raised successful children in career fields. They both also had to know and respect God because Genesis 4:3-4 reads, "And in the process of time it came to pass, that Cain brought of the fruit of the ground an offering unto the Lord. And Abel, he also brought of the firstlings of his flock and of the fat thereof. And the Lord had respect unto Abel and to his offering". Between verses 4 and 5, a shift took place within the family. We all have parents or someone who raised us, but I can see the first shift is to model Adam's role to teach our kids about God as a parent myself. If you can be honest, how many of us grew within some animosity towards our parents, wishing they would've done this or that? We grew to look at our parents instead of looking to God. Adam and Eve taught their kids to go to God as we see they did in scripture.

The second thing is to teach our children the way of life with good work ethics and to not expect handouts from the world. As you can see, no two people are the same, even in the family. Two brothers with two separate careers, but they both knew God. Adam and Eve made mistakes in their early life together, but they were successful parents. As parents, we could get so caught up with wanting our children to be better than us that we forget the important principles of God first. Without God, holidays and time with family start to become a time of just success and accolades. A time of Who has the most money and who kids are doing the best. Who do you know in the family that works hard but doesn't feel appreciated? Are you that person? Have you grown to feel not celebrated but see your other siblings or relatives being celebrated? Do you see how easy the focus can shift from work in careers first then secondly God? So, Adam and Eve weren't the problems. The shift came within the children of the family. Your problem may not have been your parents, so stop looking at them. Your problem is you! If you've grown to know God, then your responsibility towards a relationship with God is on you.

At some point, Cain and Abel shifted their focus from their earthly parent to their heavenly parent. They knew God was watching them, and they knew how to fear God. But God gives us an important clue on what happened within the family. Verse 5 reads, "But unto Cain and to his offering he had no respect." And Cain became angry, and he looked annoyed and hostile. And God said, "Why are you angry and look annoyed? If you do well and what's pleasing to me, will you not be accepted? And if you do not do well by ignoring my principles, sin crouches at your door; it desires to master you, but you must master it." Cain went on to murder his own brother and responded with an attitude when God confronted him about it. This story passage shows the outcome of murder, but that wasn't the cause. God warned him that this would eventually happen if he didn't shift his attitude. In other words, God is saying, "Cut It Out!" Adam and Eve allowed sin to enter humanity, but Cain allowed jealousy, envy, and murder into the human race. Cain did what most of us are doing, and God sees it. Cain had an attitude, and envy crept into his heart because he was comparing himself to his brother. Jealousy by comparisons is a strong root that could lead to the fruits of murdering our fellow brothers and sisters.

God is saying to you, "Cut it out!" because you have no reason to compare yourself to anyone else. You envy your brother and sisters because you're not giving your all in your work, but you want God's blessing. You're focusing too much on other people lives and not your own. "I've watched you in the field, and I'm not accepting less than what you're capable of Cain (Your Name)." Cain's attitude is what attitudes we've adopted in our families. We don't necessarily kill physically, but we kill each other in words. Hatred will cause people to stab you in the back in a heartbeat. We fight and destroy each other in families because we're trying to either keep up or talk down. We've taken our eyes off bringing our best to God first, but we rather compete in our best to family. God is saying cut it out because you can get the same type of blessings if you do what I asked you to do wholeheartedly. God sees right through you, and he knows your potential in the fields. Even though I'm writing this, I am also convicted of this same issue. We fight each other in the world just to keep up with the Jones, but my last name is Washington. Why my focus on the Jones. Why is any of our focus on the Jones? I can guarantee that Jones had family issues as well because they got a reputation to uphold. They fight to uphold their status in life because they know the world is their competition and need to keep up. Do you think if Uncle Jones is struggling with life that Cousin Jones isn't going to talk about him behind his back? Yeah, right, that's a fight waiting to happen, but you get my point.

God always desired to have a large family and wanted all his children to succeed. The problem is we misunderstood what success is in God's eyes. The world defines success as how much money you can accumulate and how much materials you own. We've gotten so caught up in the ways of the world that we've started to create idols we worship, knowingly or unknowingly. But in the family of God, the definition of success is becoming who He created you to be at your fullest potential. He doesn't want you to continue in life comparing yourself to anybody else but yourself. He tells us how to start doing this in Romans 12:1-5, "Therefore, I urge you, brothers and sisters, in view of God's mercy, to offer your bodies as a living sacrifice, holy and pleasing to God - this is your true and proper worship". Do not conform to the pattern of this world but be transformed by the renewing of your minds. Then you will be able to test and approve what God's will is. For, by the grace given to me, I say to every one of you: "Do not think of yourself more highly than you ought, but rather think of yourself with sober judgment, in accordance with the faith God has distributed to each of you. Just as each of us has one body with many members, and these members do not all have the same function, so, in Christ, we, though are many, form one body, and each member belongs to all the others".

God wants you to know who he created you to be by understanding who you are in his family. Let me give you an illustration to help you understand more. Let's say I buy you a pack of knives, and this pack represents the family of God. This pack didn't cost you anything, but you represent one of these knives inside. No two knives are the same. The variety comes in different shapes and sizes. To understand an individual knifes' job, we must look and see how it is designed and cut. To understand who you are in Gods pack, you first must renew your mind on who you really are. In other words, how are you cut and designed? What gifts and functions are you aware of that God placed inside you? Remember, we're not comparing ourselves, but do you notice any resemblance with other talents and gifts. God may put you in similar situations to admire someone else talents, but it's just to make you aware of something in you. Your talent or gift may look the same, but to what degree? The knife is in a pack - they all are shiny, they all have teeth, but they all don't have the same jobs.

One knife job is to chop; the next is just to slice. Another is just to dice. When you think about preparations for cooking, you need different utensils to get specific jobs done. You're not going to use a small knife to try and split a watermelon, right? And you don't need a butcher knife to cut up onions. The knives don't have a problem comparing themselves to each other because they're aware of who they are and what they're capable of doing. Don't be ashamed because God designed you as a butter knife. You see, a butter knife barely has sharp teeth. So, we can easily see its job is not to cut. God needs you to take care of spreading. When you heat up, the butter doesn't stand a chance. Why would you think God called you to split this melon when you're designed to spread this bread? This doesn't make sense, correct? So, instead of focusing on a competition with the next man, focus on how you're cut and designed.

Cain and Abel had two different jobs but were in the same family. You and I have two different jobs, but we're in the same family. I don't have to compete against you and be jealous of what you have because you used what God gave you. Our jobs are to know God, know who we are in him, and give our best at what we're designed to do. That's all God wants from us. Remember this even if you don't get anything else from the other chapters! All the knives in the pack come in different shapes and sizes, but they all have a few things in common. They're all sharp and dangerous! You have something in common with your fellow brothers and sisters in the kingdom; we're all sharp and dangerous! Renew your minds to that, and the Enemies don't stand a chance!!!!!

CHAPTER EIGHT
I Want Out

"Whatever I tell you in the dark, speak in the light; and what you hear in the ear, preach on the housetops", Matthew 10:27. These are the words of Jesus to instruct his disciples. My experience with God helped me realize that he gives warning or instructions before anything He does or allows happen. As you have read, most of my experiences came to me in the dark. Its pros and cons to darkness. We usually lie down in darkness. We try to get rest from life in darkness. It's a time to be still and listen. We can't read in the dark, but we can still hear the dark. Darkness is a time of discipline. We usually associate darkness with evil, but God is near the dark. Exodus 20:21, "The people remained at a distance, while Moses approached the thick darkness where God was." Some of us still fear and run from the dark. We run because darkness also represents ignorance.

You're afraid of what you don't understand - some confused darkness with light. We think what we see is all there is to our natural eyes, and that's considered light. The spiritual thing to the natural eye is darkness to us, but it's backward. What you see came from the unseen. The word of God is like our lamp to see into the Spirit. I was trying to see and understand in the dark, and the revelations I've experienced caused me to run in fear. I wanted to run out; I wanted nothing to do with it. I was trying to find a door of escape, but all I needed was to turn the lamp on inside me.

I know now I wasn't the only one running from God. Jonah the Prophet had a run-out experience with God. You know the saying, "You can run, but you can't hide." God knows where you are at all times, and Jonah could not escape the call of God on his life. If God calls you, how far do you think you can run? Jonah story is a little different from the rest of the prophets. Jonah already knew God, and he ran with an attitude. God gave Jonah a message to go to the people in Nineveh and tell them to repent from their wickedness. Jonah carried a message inside of him but ran in the opposite direction from the delivery point. Jonah was saying, "I want out!" Jonah did not want anything to do with the people and wanted God to punish them for their evil ways. He was thinking God doesn't allow a lot of evil to carry on before he finally comes with his judgement. But when God commissioned him, He knew that God would show mercy and forgive them if they repented. I personally can understand Jonah because we see a lot of evil that people do now in the world, and it seems like they're getting away with it. But that's the difference between man and God. Jonah ran in the opposite direction and boarded a ship to Tarshish. Eventually, a storm broke out, and the other crew members were confused about why Jonah wasn't helping to fight against the storm.

The crew members were all in the dark, but Jonah knew the truth inside him the whole time. He knew this storm broke out because he was running from God, and the people around him were suffering because of him. That's a message in itself. Jonah admitted that if they threw him overboard that the storm would cease. So they threw him overboard, and the storm ceased. A huge fish swallowed Jonah in the middle of the sea, and Jonah was in isolation inside the fish belly. He was praying and sat in there for three days and three nights. It's funny that you see "mess" at the beginning of the word "message". Jonah was in a mess because he was carrying a message. But Jonah prayed because he wanted Out! God wanted Jonah out because he wanted the message Out!

Jonah can represent us, and as I shared in my Introduction, I too experienced being inside the fish belly for exactly three days and three nights. I didn't have a good relationship with God back then, but I did know I needed to pray. The mess I was in taught me how to pray and pray hard. Looking back on it, that fish represented the systems in this world where it seems we can't get out unless it's by the grace of God. You may think, "Well, God hasn't called me to deliver a word or anything like that, but he has called you to righteousness". He's watching and wants you to live right and do things honestly. God had already warned me about this money before I got caught with it. I was carrying the warning message before I was in the mess. But me being ignorant, I didn't recognize his voice speaking, and I was confident not to get caught. I guarantee if you're doing something you have no business doing, God already warned you about it. You're either not paying attention to him or you're disregarding his message until the boat rocks or the fish swallow you. I never knew that the mess would become a message eventually. I was praying hard to God to get me out of jail, but God allowed me to be out because he wanted what was in me out.

Jonah also represented life inside the belly. Your real life is inside your belly. The real you is inside of you, and it is deep below. There are a lot of activities going on in the deep that you can't see. Think about how deep the oceans are. The deeper you go, the darker it gets. When you get saved, where do you think the Holy Spirit lives? How dark do you think it was inside a fish? Jonah couldn't see a thing, but he prayed in the dark. When the baptism of the Holy spirit comes, the Bible says he comes in fire. Well, that fire is happening within the belly. When the Holy Spirit came to baptize me, he warned me in the word that I would feel pain, but I wouldn't experience it again. When I saw it, I didn't understand what I was reading until three days later, when the process began. I experienced a pain in my belly that words can't explain. I have a deeper understanding of what fasting does with the body and the Spirit because of this experience. I only craved fruits, and the thought of anything cooked or dead to eat made me want to puke. During this process, the spiritual warfare was crazy.

Satan was trying his best to get me to commit suicide during this period. I felt the demonic presence rest right on the top of my head. Everywhere I went, I could not escape it. He has a funny way of showing up when you're vulnerable. This experience was awful; I was in a battle in my head but feeling the fire in my belly. My question was, "Lord, how long is this going to last?" This experience went on for about a week and a half. For some reason, about the fourth or fifth day, I've gotten immune to it. I was still feeling the burning pain inside, but I started picking up spiritual messages everywhere. I can remember watching T.V., and the man said, "Free your mind and let the Spirit work". I tried not to pay attention to all that because I was still in a state of confusion, but the warfare seemed to stop, and I started feeling a little stronger inside. By the end of the next week, the process was over. I felt the glory of God rested on my head as if He crowned me with a halo. This glory felt so good and powerful that it filled my whole soul. I felt like my whole body was illuminated, and I was purified. Just think of it this way, the Holy Spirit came inside you and rearranged some furniture, threw out some trash, and restrained your floors. He comes inside to deep clean the filthiness you allowed from the outside. He has your real pictures on the walls, showing who you will become. He has a map planned out on the table for you to follow. He made his bed in the basement bedroom, and he's reclining in his chair, waiting for you to call him up for help. He's in your neighborhood, and the house may seem quiet, but someone is living on the inside.

Like Jonah, I was trying to run away from what I was holding. God said to me, "I Want Out"! Everything I've experienced was not just for me but for the world to know. God gave me a commission years ago, and he confirmed it in His word to me. Some things I explained in this book are wrapped up in this scripture - Acts 26:16-18, "Stand on your feet". I have chosen you to be my servant. That is why I appeared to you; you must tell other people about what you have seen. After that, I will show you other things you must tell people. I will send you to speak about me to Jews and Gentiles. Some of them will want to hurt you. But I will keep you safe. You will help them to understand what is true. They are like people who live in the dark. Teach them what is true about me. Then they will be like people who live in the light. Now Satan has power over them. Lead them from there into God's kingdom. Then God will forgive them for the wrong things that they have done. Because they believe in me, God will accept them as His own people.

Jonah was told a message in the dark to speak in the light. I experienced things in the dark to tell in the light. Trying to become an author was never on the agenda with my life. I was always trying to run in another direction but never escaped what I was holding. I have more experiences to share that has nothing to do with Static. God wanted me to title this "Static" because people only hear static when He tries to speak. Like myself, he had to speak in the dark the most because I never took time to listen in daylight hours. If you took the time to read this, trust that you will probably experience some of these encounters. If you do, I would love to hear about it in your book or see it on your social media. The call of God is from the inside out, not the other way round. You don't chase God; you follow God. God placed everything inside of you, and he calls it out. Your job is to go inside and see what and who is in there. May God bless your journey, and I hope to hear from you soon.

www.ingramcontent.com/pod-product-compliance
Lightning Source LLC
Chambersburg PA
CBHW050443010526
44118CB00013B/1654